THE MOST AMAZING SOCCER STORIES OF ALL TIME
FOR KIDS!

MICHAEL LANGDON

itsmikelangdon

© Copyright 2023 - All rights reserved.

The content contained within this book may not be reproduced, duplicated or transmitted without direct written permission from the author or the publisher.

Under no circumstances will any blame or legal responsibility be held against the publisher, or author, for any damages, reparation, or monetary loss due to the information contained within this book, either directly or indirectly.

Legal Notice:

This book is copyright protected. It is only for personal use. You cannot amend, distribute, sell, use, quote or paraphrase any part, or the content within this book, without the consent of the author or publisher.

Disclaimer Notice:

Please note the information contained within this document is for educational and entertainment purposes only. All effort has been executed to present accurate, up to date, reliable, complete information. No warranties of any kind are declared or implied. Readers acknowledge that the author is not engaged in the rendering of legal, financial, medical or professional advice. The content within this book has been derived from various sources. Please consult a licensed professional before attempting any techniques outlined in this book.

By reading this document, the reader agrees that under no circumstances is the author responsible for any losses, direct or indirect, that are incurred as a result of the use of the information contained within this document, including, but not limited to, errors, omissions, or inaccuracies.

Dedication

To Tills, Charlie, Lily & Poppy with love.
Thank you for the inspiration.

Before You Start

This book is produced with ♥ for children everywhere in the USA.

As it was originally written for a global audience, you will find that we call soccer "football" throughout the book.

Please know that we mean soccer in those instances – the same beautiful game that unites us all.

Table of Contents

The Tiny Bird With Bent Legs	6
That's Just Scilly! The World's Smallest League	8
A Rush of Blood to The Head	10
The Psychic Octopus	12
Absolutely Dental!	14
A Flying Header	16
Making a Dog's Dinner Out of it	18
Triple Word Sore	20
The Scorpion Kick	22
The Lionesses	24
I Can't See You in Grey	26
Pizza-gate	28
I Can Give You a Hand - literally	30
The Game of Three Halves	32

Pickles The Dog And The Missing World Cup	34
The Goal That Was "Like a UFO Landing"	36
A Very Public World Cup Poo	38
The Lisbon Lions	40
Villan's Villain Four Goal Fest	42
Football's Greatest Fairytale	44
Zombie Footballers? The World's Longest Match	46
Blink And You'll Miss it - Fastest Goals in The World	48
Sardine Spectator Record—Most Fans in a Stadium	50
The Most Amount of Goals Ever	52
Bury Me in My Boots—I'll Never Hang Them Up!	54
Ali Dia - Football's Biggest Fraudster	56
A Truly Golden Goal	58
Ice Cream, You Scream, we All Scream!	60
The Greatest Cup Run in The World	62

The Tiny Bird With Bent Legs

Once upon a time, in the land of magical footballers (Brazil), a small boy was born. The boy was so small that he looked like a wren.

A wren is one of the smallest birds to live on planet Earth. And this boy was so incredibly tiny, that his parents called him "Tiny Little Wren," Or "Garrincha," in his native Portuguese.

Garrincha wasn't like the other boys. Not only was he tiny, but he also had one leg that was bent, and it was much shorter than his other leg.

It seemed as if his small stature and bent legs would stop him from achieving his dream of playing football. However, his passion for football was so strong that he achieved some of the most incredible feats ever seen in the sport!

"Garrincha could do things with the ball that no other player could," said Pele, the best player of all time.

Garrincha went on to become one of the most feared footballing players of his time, leading Brazil to the 1958 and 1962 World Cup titles and being named player of the tournament AND top scorer in the 1962 World Cup.

Garrincha had it all. The Chilean journalists at the 1962 world cup were so impressed by his football ability, that they thought he actually came from another planet!

Off the football pitch he also did extraordinary things. One of the things he is famous for is having 22 children!

That's Just Scilly! The World's Smallest Football League

There is a tiny group of islands in the southwest of England called the Scilly Isles - it is home to only 2000 people.

Their love for football on the island is so strong that they started a football league - with only two teams in it!

And while the football might not be of the same standard as the Premier League, the Scilly Isles football league offers its own brand of charm.

The league competition involves the Woolpack Wanderers and the Garrison Gunners playing each other 18 times throughout the season.

It may not be the most exciting league in the world, but the beauty of this competition is that if you play for one of the teams, there is always a 50/50 chance of becoming champions of Scilly!

Games are often on a Sunday, and luckily for the players who don't like travelling, the games are always on the same pitch.

Another perk of playing football in the Scilly Isles, is that if at any time one of the teams is running away with the league, then there are always cup competitions to look forward to.

Two domestic cup competitions (The Wholesalers Cup and the Foredeck Cup) also take place in Scilly, and the long and arduous route to the final is always contested by the same two teams.

As if that wasn't enough, the football association of Scilly also puts on a Charity Shield competition as the season's first game.

And the two teams to compete in the Charity Shield? You guessed it. Woolpack Wanderers and the Garrison Gunners.

A Rush of Blood to The Head

This is the story of Zinedine Zidane's last ever game of football.

Zizou, as he was affectionately called, had the craziest final game of any football player in the world.

The biggest game in world football comes round once every four years. It is the World Cup final, and one BILLION people watch the game live.

In the final of Germany 2006, Zizou scored a 'Panenka' penalty kick. A Panenka is a cheeky and unexpected dink of the ball that only the bravest of footballers ever dare to think about, let alone execute.

That alone would be reason to celebrate the day. But it is what happened a few minutes later that will forever be remembered.

With Italy and France tied at 1-1, and the game just about to go to penalties, Italian defender Marco Materazzi and Zinedine Zidane had a coming together on the pitch. Nothing unusual - just part of the game.

A few words were spoken, and BANG! Zizou exploded in a fit of anger.

In what can only be described as the biggest "red-rag-to-a-bull" moment in football history, Zizou threw himself, head-first, into the chest of Materazzi.

The referee missed the incident but his assistant didn't. After a private chat between the two, the referee had no option but to send him off minutes before the penalty shootout.

Paul The Psychic Octopus

During the World Cup in South Africa in 2010, it wasn't a footballer who was the star of the show, it was a psychic octopus!

When it comes to guessing the future, there are many different methods that people use to try and predict the future. Some use tarot cards, others palm read, some even use tea leaves to guess what's ahead.

One of the most unusual methods is using an octopus.

Paul the psychic octopus became famous for his ability to correctly predict the outcomes of football matches, including the 2010 World Cup final in which Spain became champions.

So how did he do it? Paul, who lived in a tank in Germany, would be fed from two boxes that were draped in the flags of the countries that were playing a match that day.

Whichever box he opened first would be deemed as his prediction as to which country would win the game.

In July 2010, Germany were playing Spain in the semi-final of the World Cup. That morning, Paul chose to have his breakfast from a box draped in a Spanish flag instead of the one draped in the German flag - he broke millions of German hearts that morning.

Later on that day, and as foretold by one of the greatest psychics the world has ever seen, Germany went on to lose the semifinal 1-0.

Paul always guessed correctly during that World Cup. He had the finest performance of 2010, and won the hearts of millions of football fans on every continent on earth.

Absolutely M/Dental!

A referee in Denmark couldn't blow his whistle for full time after he misplaced something very important.

You would be forgiven for thinking that the referee lost his whistle, but no, it was actually his teeth that he lost!

As is often the case with older people, they need fake teeth to replace their real teeth. This happens when they haven't taken care of their teeth growing up.

These fake teeth are called dentures, and Danish referee Henning Erikstrup had a lovely pair of dentures.

One day, he was refereeing a game between Ebeltoft and Norager. As he was running to keep up with the players, his teeth flew out of his mouth!

In the time it took him to find his teeth and put them back in his mouth, Ebeltoft scored a last minute equaliser!

After a few seconds of searching for his teeth, he eventually found them! Once he put them in his mouth, he blew the whistle and people thought it was the end of the game.

Astonishingly, he blew to disallow Ebeltoft's last minute goal! The Ebeltoft players complained to him.

Erikstrup simply told them the truth. That he had wanted to end the game before they scored, but he couldn't announce because at the time he had no teeth!

Ebeltoft protested against the result to the Danish Football Association - but the country's FA stood by their referee and Norager kept their win.

A Flying Header

"Flying headers" are scored all the time in football. That is what we say when a player leaps in the air and makes contact with the football using their head.

As far as we are aware, there is only one ACTUAL flying header to have ever been scored in a game of football. And that accolade goes to an unknown seagull in Manchester, England.

At the beginning of the 1999 season, Stalybridge Celtic Colts were playing Hollingworth Juniors in a local league in the north of England.

During the game, 13-year-old striker Danny Worthington took a shot towards goal that went really high. He missed the goal by a mile - the ball went so high that it was close to hitting a cloud!

It was as the ball kept going skyward that one of the most unusual things ever seen on a football field happened.

By this point, Danny had already turned away in disgust at how rubbish his attempt on goal had been. Shoulders slumped, he was about to apologise to his teammates for the shot, when they all started running towards him. They were celebrating a goal!

Tuning back to find the ball in the back of the net, Danny put his arms in the air and joined in the celebrations too. He had no idea how the ball had ended up there, but that wasn't going to stop him from celebrating!

He turned out to be celebrating an assist.

That's right, Danny got credited with an assist and the official goal went to a random seagull that was flying over the penalty spot.

Danny's looping shot hit the seagull as the bird was swooping down. The ball bounced off the bird and into the back of the net!

Making a Dog's Dinner Out of it

You could be forgiven for thinking that birds were the only animals to score on the football pitch. However, there are countless tales of man's best friend getting on the scoresheet.

The most famous of these occasions must be the goal scored for Deportivo San Miguel de Rio Viejo during a Chilean football game in 2021.

As San Miguel lined up to take a free kick on the edge of the area, they called up their most trusted headers of the ball - most noticeably their centre backs.

What the opposition (Real Zaragoza) didn't know was that they had a secret weapon up their sleeve.

As the free kick was taken, an Alsatian cleverly beat the offside trap to head into the bottom left corner of the net - leaving Real Zaragoza's goalkeeper rooted to the spot.

A notable mention for another great pooch on a football field story must go to one of the greatest saves ever seen. One that would make even Peter Schmeichel be proud of. After all, he is the Great Dane!

The scene was Greater Glasgow, and Vale of Leven AFC and Ferguslie Star were battling it out in the AFL President's Cup match. It was a winner-takes-all affair.

Vale of Leven ended up winning the game 3-2, so you can imagine how angry Ferguslie striker Ross Hamilton was when he beat the offside trap, latched onto a long ball, and slotted past the keeper only to find his shot blocked by a dog having a good ol' sniff at the near post.

Annoyingly for Ferguslie Star, the ball rebounded off the dog and landed at the feet of one of their strikers who scored, but the referee ruled the goal out because of the dog's interference and gave the Leven goalkeeper a drop ball.

Triple Word Sore

There have been some crazy injuries in the history of football.

Like the time English international goalkeeper David Seaman got injured as he stretched for the remote controller in his bed.

Or there's the story of Danish Liverpool goalkeeper Michael Stensgaard who dislocated his shoulder as he was pulling down an ironing board. Stensgaard sadly had to retire because of this injury.

The craziest silly injury has got to go to Lionel Letiz.

In 2002 The French goalkeeper injured his back whilst playing the very physical game that is scrabble.

Yup, the very same game that great grandmothers around the world play in comfy sofas for hours on end.

As the French goalkeeper was playing the board game, a couple of tiles fell on the floor.

It was as he bent over to pick them up that he pulled some muscles in his back. He was out injured for quite some time and never really recovered to his previous best.

An honourable mention for a bizarre injury must go to Darius Vasell of England, who tried to alleviate a blister in his toe by drilling through his toenail with an electric power drill.

This was an incredibly silly thing to do, and he then had to go to hospital to get his foot fixed.

The Scorpion Kick

Football is an exciting sport, but most of the time, you roughly know what is going to happen.

Rene Higuita was a goalkeeper who didn't like it when people "roughly knew" what was going to happen during a game.

He was an entertainer trapped in a footballer's body.

He would often try and take on the opposition by himself, ball still at his feet, despite being the last person defending his goal. Something his teammates didn't like.

He wanted to entertain people so much that he also started scoring goals. The footballing world had rarely seen a goalkeeper who would take free kicks and penalties - but Higuita made it famous. He actually scored a healthy 41 goals in his career!

With crazy hair to match his crazy personality, it was on September 6 1995, that he wrote his name into the history books. Colombia were playing England at the 'Home' of football, Wembley stadium in London. During the game, Jamie Redknapp lobbed a ball into the goalmouth - an easy catch for any goalkeeper.

"I could catch it safely…" Higuita probably thought.
Then he remembered he was an entertainer. "Nah, let's go down in history!"

Instead of catching the ball (like anyone else would), the goalkeeper decided to throw himself in front of the ball, contort himself in mid air in the shape of a scorpion, and use his 'stinger' (his two legs arching over his back) to clear the ball out of his area.

The English football commentator of the game was obviously not expecting that - "Goodness me!" he shrieked.

The next day, in every playground in every country, school children across the world were trying this move.

Never again has a keeper attempted this audacious move during a game.

The Lionesses

It is not often that a single game of football can change a whole country.

But that's exactly what happened on July 31 2022 when England beat Germany 2-1 to win the Women's European Championship.

England had gone over 50 years without any major international victories in the sport. For everyone in the country, it was 50 years too long.

When it came to football, English people were very sad.

The whole country lived with a hopeless dream that football would one day "come home".

The thing was that 'one day' didn't really seem like it was ever going to come. Until the last day of July in the summer of 2022.

The Lionesses did what no other English team had done in 56 years. They beat Germany in a final and gave England their first senior football trophy of the 21st century.

What the lionesses did for the country, and most importantly, for millions of young fans across the country was immeasurable. They united the country at a time when it was going through a bad time.

They gave everyone in the country hope, joy and pride.

At a time when a lot of people thought men's football was better than women's football, the Lionesses victory changed that forever.

Never again would women's football be seen as anything but equal to that of their male's counterpart.

A huge change to the way the country thought, and a testament to the grit, passion and determination those girls showed for their country that summer.

I Can't See You in Grey

On April 13 1996 Manchester United played Southampton at The Dell. At the end of the first half, United found themselves 3-0 down.

United players went into the dressing room wearing grey and came back out wearing blue and white stripes.

Their manager's idea to win the game was to change the colour of the kit that his players were wearing! He hoped that this would turn the game around and see them rescue at least a draw from the game.

The team could not recover in the second half and they were beaten by Southampton in the end.

The only thing more embarrassing than the scoreline was the excuse their manager, Alex Ferguson, made for the loss. He claimed that the players couldn't pick each other out on the pitch because of the colour of the kit - and that had been the reason why he'd ordered his troops to change kit at half time.

People laughed at the time, but apparently Ferguson had been in touch with "eye scientists" at the time.

The advice from the professionals was that grey was one of the hardest colours the human eye could see. As such Ferguson kept a second kit on standby whenever they played in grey - just in case!

On that day when United had an awful first half, Ferguson thought it was down to the kit and quickly rectified it at halftime.

The world saw it as an outrageous excuse, but, two decades later it was discovered that there was science to the madness.

Not that it mattered, United went on to lose 3-1 and were fined £10,000 by the English Football Association for changing kits at half time.

In Ferguson's defence, you could argue that they won the second half 1-0.

Talking about Ferguson, there's a great story that originates from Old Trafford in Manchester.

The year was 2004 and Arsenal were visiting Manchester United on a run of being unbeaten for 49 games.

Arsenal players were gloating about the fact that the 50th unbeaten game would be achieved at the home of their bitter rivals. United didn't quite like that.

The game was tense and physical. Ruud Van Nistelrooy was lucky to be on the pitch after a bad challenge on Ashley Cole. He then scored a goal to add salt into Arsenal's wound.

The Gunners went on to lose their unbeaten streak and all hell broke loose after full time in the tunnel on the way back to the changing rooms.

A full fight broke out, things were surely going to get considerably out of hand when a pizza was thrown across the tunnel, landing flat on Alex Ferguson's face.

It dribbled down his cheek and onto his elegant suit. Time stood still.

Pushing people around, despite not being very nice at all, was somewhat acceptable when emotions were running high.

However, covering the most successful British manager in marinara sauce was a step too far. Ferguson retired to the changing room, and the players – feeling like they had really let down the headmaster – followed soon after.

For years after the event, the British press tried to discover who the culprit of this cowardly act had been. The investigation (creatively dubbed 'pizza-gate'), led nowhere.

It wasn't until a few years, in a radio phone interview, that Martin Keown revealed that the person who threw the pizza had been none other than Cesc Fabregas.

"I Can Give You a Hand" Literally

In 1906 in Argentina, Barracas FC lost their goalkeeper to bitter rivals Alumni FC. With an upcoming game against Estudiantes, Barracas were scrambling to find a goalkeeper.

As is often the case, one of their defenders stepped up and offered his services in between the sticks.

"I can give you a hand", Winston Coe said. "You know I can't give you two", he said jokingly. Winston Coe only had one arm.

With the game only round the corner, Barracas FC found themselves in a bit of a pickle. They had to say yes. Coe went in between the sticks for the game against Estudiantes, and both fans and players were gobsmacked by Coe's performance on the day.

The Argentinean press praised him for his confidence and shot stopping ability (apparently he saved quite a few shots that day).

Estudiantes beat Barracas 2-1 despite Coe's heroic efforts, but his performance was so good that Barracas kept him in goal for their next two games.

Unfortunately for Barracas, they went on to lose 11-0 against Reformer and 5-0 against an Alumni side that had their former goalkeeper in the team.

Imagine how he felt when he walked out onto the pitch and realised he'd been replaced with a man with one arm?!

Despite the two beatings, the Argentine press concluded that the results would have been "catastrophic" had Coe not been in goal.

With three games under his belt, Winston Coe not only taught the world a lesson in determination, he also gifted us one of the most feel-good football stories out there!

The Game of Three Halves

In the opening game of the English 1894/95 football season, referee Thomas Kirkham, was late for kick-off.

Not that it mattered. Everyone trusted a Mr. John Conqueror to take his place until the referee arrived.

It was hard not to trust him with a surname like that!

Conqueror was happy to volunteer his services, and the game between Derby County and Sunderland began.

Derby County didn't start well. They conceded 3 goals in the first 45 minutes.

Conqueror blew for half-time and handed the whistle over to Thomas Kirkham, the original referee who had arrived 45 minutes late!

It was at this point that this game would go down as one of the most incredible games in the history of the sport.

Kirkham asked the Derby team if they would not prefer to start the game from the very beginning? Losing by 3 goals, their answer was obvious.

The little boy tasked with hanging the numbers on the scoreboard had to take down the "3" under Sunderland and put up a fresh "0" under both Sunderland and Visitors.

Mr. T Kirkham started the entire 90 minutes over again!

Sunderland kept to their original game plan. So much so that by the end of the "second half", the little boy had hung up 3-0 to Sunderland once again.

The players went into the dressing room for their second half time break and came out to battle their way through a "third half".

Sunderland, fired by a sense of injustice perhaps, were ruthless. That little boy ended up hanging five more goals for Sunderland, with a 8-0 victory for the Black Cats.

Pickles The Dog And The Missing World Cup

England hosted and won the World Cup in the summer of 1966. They were also very lucky to have a trophy to lift at the end of the event.

On the 20th of March, a few weeks before the beginning of the tournament, the trophy disappeared from Westminster's Central Hall, where it had been on display to the public.

The following day, the police received a ransom note demanding £15,000 in £1 and £5 notes if they wanted the trophy back.

As the police prepared a complicated operation to get the trophy back (it included printing fake notes), an unlikely new hero emerged: Pickles the black and white collie dog.

As Pickles went for his Sunday walkies in Beulah Park, South East London on the 27th of March 1966 he stopped to sniff a package wrapped in newspaper. It was lying next to the front wheel of a parked car.

Pickles' owner, upon unwrapping it, must have been gobsmacked to discover it was the missing World Cup!

His owner received the equivalent of £100,000 in today's money as a reward for finding the trophy, but it was arguably Pickles who gained more value from the find.

Not only did Pickles get awarded the silver medal of the National Canine Defence League, but he got invited to England's celebration banquet after the team won the World Cup.

He also starred in film and television shows for the remainder of the year and won multiple "Dog of the Year" awards.

He will always be known as the dog who rescued the World Cup.

The Goal That Was "Like a UFO Landing"

Depending on who you ask, aliens and UFOs don't exist.

This is because they are so rare that only very few people have ever apparently seen them.

So when a manager says that a goal was "like a UFO landing," you know something extraordinary has happened!

It was September 2008 and Watford FC were playing against Reading FC.

In the 15th minute of the game at Vicarage Road, Reading fired in a corner. The play continued FIVE METRES away from the goal line, when, out of nowhere, the referee blew his whistle!

To the astonishment of everyone, the referee gave a goal to Reading. Everyone in the ground was gobsmacked (Reading players included!).

The ball had been so far away from the goalline that everyone thought the referee was joking.

When they realised he wasn't, many Watford players were very angry.

Furore ensued and the Referee red carded Aidy Boothroyd, the Watford manager, for dissent.

Watford managed to claw back the deficit to 2-1, but unfortunately a late penalty to Reading meant the match ended 2-2 (despite the ball only crossing the line 3 times).

A disgruntled Aidy Boothroyd, when questioned about the goal after the game, said: "I could not believe it. It was like a UFO had just landed."

A Very Public World Cup Poo

Gary Lineker is the English darling of football.

The ex-England-striker-turned-TV-pundit is one of the most liked presenters in England.

In fact, he is so liked that he can get away with pooing in front of 35,000 people, wiping his bottom and hands on the grass, and still going on to earn the love and admiration of his fellow countrymen and women.

It was 1990 and England were playing Ireland in a World Cup group game in Italy. Lineker had a brilliant start, scoring a goal in under ten minutes. However, unbeknownst to his fans, he was playing with an upset tummy.

In the second half he tried to control a ball that was passed in the air to him. He collapsed on the floor under a challenge from an Irish defender, and whilst sitting up on the ground, did a weird sort of 'break dance' on his bum.

He then ran to the opposition's area and wiped his hands on the grass.

This was all before continuing through to the semi finals of the World Cup, where England lost to Germany. Lineker established himself as a world class striker en route to the semi-final.

It wasn't until two decades later, that the seemingly innocuous 'break dance on his bum' that was caught by TV cameras, took on a new meaning.

Lineker confessed to the world that he couldn't control his diarrhoea that day in 1990, and he accidentally pooed himself whilst stretching for the ball.

The quick thinking attacker quickly slid on his bum to clear the mess, and did the same with his hands as he ran to receive the ensuing free kick.

It's no wonder that defenders couldn't get anywhere near him that tournament. The smell probably put them off!

The Lisbon Lions

Imagine grabbing all your neighbourhood mates for a game of football and ending up winning the biggest club competition in the world.

That's exactly what Celtic FC did in 1967.

That year Celtic won the European Cup. No biggie, right? There have been dozens of teams to have done that since.

However, what makes Celtic FC's achievement of 1967 so mind-blowingly good, is that all of their players that season were born within 30 miles of their home ground, Celtic Park.

Bobby Lennox was the person born the furthest away, and he only lived an hour away by bus!

A group of lads, all born close by, taking on and slaying European Giants, is the stuff of Hollywood films.

In the summer of 1967, the 15 Scotsmen travelled to Lisbon to line up against the mighty Inter Milan in the final of the European Cup.

The Italian giants were looking to take home yet another European Cup (having won two in the previous three finals) and took the lead in the first half.

Celtic fought back, and scored twice to beat Inter 2-1.

"There is not a prouder man on God's Earth than me at this moment", said Jock Stein, Celtic Manager on the day.

It's a pride that has continued for over 50 years Celtic Park, and one which, given the global scale of the modern game, will never be repeated again.

Villan's Villain Four Goal Fest

There are only very few things in football that are more satisfying than scoring a hat-trick. One of those things is perhaps scoring 4 goals instead of 3.

That is exactly what Chris Nicholl did for Aston Villa in 1976 when they played Leicester City at Filbert Street.

And whilst there have been many players since Nicholl who have bagged four or more goals in one game, what rocketed Nicholl into the record books is that the game he scored all four goals in ended up a 2-2 draw!

A skilled centre back, Chris Nicholl often got on the scoresheet. He is often remembered for a 25 yard screamer that he scored against Everton in the 1977 League Cup final.

However, it is the performance in the game against Leicester that will forever make him a household legend.

Twice he put the opposition in front, and twice he made amends by clawing back the deficit that he had single-handedly imposed on his team.

After the game, Nicholl asked the referee for the ball to commemorate the event. The referee politely declined as it was his only ball (how times have changed!)

Interestingly, it was not the first time a player had scored two goals and two own goals in a game.

Sam Wynne did exactly the same thing for Oldham Athletic against Manchester United back in 1923 - although that game ended up as a 3-2 Victory to Odlham!

It seems lightning can strike twice (or eight times) on a football pitch!

Football's Greatest Fairytale

A story of fantastical forces and beings, with fighters & villains, and unlikely heroes in the making. Such are the ingredients of a fairytale.

In August 2015, bookmakers across the world thought that there was more chance of finding a mythical monster in the depths of Loch Ness, than there was of Leicester City FC winning the Premier League.

Nine months later, one of those two things became a reality.

Leicester's journey started gripping the whole world around February 2016. It was at this point that the team's position in the league (they cemented the top position after beating title favourites Manchester City) could no longer be seen as a fluke.

The world was gripped - every neutral fan in the world wanted them to continue fighting against all odds, and stay top for a few more games.

The players, who had come from humble football origins, were not only competing in the toughest league in the world, they were beating the richest clubs in the world.

Week in and week out, Leicester would go on to brush aside whatever team was put in front of them, and it was clear to see that legends were being made.

Future World Cup winners like N'golo Kanté were emerging, and other talents like Riyad Mahrez were lighting up the league with their skill.

Like a soap opera that grips a nation, the feel good story continued every weekend, until May 2nd 2016, when other games in the league mathematically confirmed that Leicester City would be champions of England.

Out of the 38 fixtures that season they won 23, drew 12, and lost only three! They were the giant-killers of the decade, if not the century.

People the world over were in delirium. The most epic of underdog sagas had just been completed. To top it off, it had all been overseen by their leader Claudio Ranieri, the most charismatic old man, the kind of grandfather everyone's always wanted to have.

Zombie Footballers? The World's Longest Match

In 2019 a group of amateur football players decided to break a record for the longest football game ever played.

To do this, they played continuously in a mind-numbing and strength-sapping football match that lasted 169 hours!

That's one week and 1 hour of continuous football.

Playing football is any fan's dream, but doing anything continuously for over a week would surely test your resolve.

Tempers frayed and tears were shed in the course of the marathon, as players stumbled on for hour after hour, day after day.

But the play had to go on uninterrupted if they wanted to break the record.

The teams were aiming to beat the Guinness World record of 134 hours, but as they played, the distressing news came in that a German side had played for 168 hours.

So, they played grimly onwards for the extra day and a half.

The scoreline ended up at 988-951, and luckily for everyone involved, it was safely beyond the need for a penalty shootout!

Cancer research was the real winner at the end of the week, with the charity Kicking Off Against Cancer raising thousands of pounds through their efforts.

Blink And You'll Miss it

The quickest goal ever recorded by the English Football Association was scored by Marc Burrows.

The English striker was playing for Cowes Sports Reserves against Eastleigh when, in 2004, he took a shot immediately after kick off.

Aided by some strong winds, the shot rocketed into the back of the opposition's net an impressive 2.56 seconds after kick off.

Nawaf Al Abed of Saudi Arabia claims to have scored in 2 seconds for Al Hilal against Al Shoalah, however his time has never been officially recorded by the Guiness Book of World Records.

There is little to no video evidence of the above two goals, so an honourable mention must go to Gavin Stokes of Maryhill FC, who wins the award of 'fastest-goal-where-there-is-plenty-of-video-evidence-for'.

After the Ballon D'or, that's the most coveted award in world football.

In 2017, Maryhill FC were facing Clydebank FC in a Scottish semi-professional league.

The Clydebank goalie was still adjusting his gloves when a looping shot straight from kick off by Stokes went past his head with only 3.2 seconds on the clock.

The fastest youth goal on record was delivered in a 2012 match in Serbia, when Dorcol's Vuk Bakic teed off to score a stunner against Polet. It stopped the clock at 2.2 seconds, beating Mark Burrows' previous record score for Cowes Sports Reserves against Eastleigh by a few seconds.

Bakic's goal is also very popular on YouTube and it makes for some great viewing for everyone – apart from the opposing goalkeeper.

Most Fans in a Stadium

In 1923 Wembley Stadium hosted its first ever match: The FA Cup final between Bolton Wanderers and West Ham United.

The game drew a sell-out crowd of 126,000. However, about another 180,000 spectators made their way into the stadium.

In the end, it is estimated that there were about 300,000 human beings packed inside Wembley Stadium that late April afternoon in 1923. (300,022 if you include the players on the pitch!)

The game had to be postponed for 45 minutes as the crowd spilled onto the playing field and didn't allow play to start.

That was easily fixed by the police though, who carelessly came round on horses and crammed the pitch invaders back into the stands. Miraculously, nobody got hurt; and Bolton won their first ever FA Cup that day.

The official record for the most fans in one game, however, goes to the Maracana Stadium in Brazil. Uruguay was being hosted by Brazil for the 1950 World Cup final. Interest was at fever pitch, resulting in 199,854 people cramming into the stadium!

Twelve winners' medals had been made in advance and inscribed with the Brazilian team's names. The local press had even published a newspaper edition with the banner headline "Brazil: World Champions!!!"

Unfortunately for Brazil, Uruguay went on to win 2-1. It's safe to say that the match also holds the record for the highest numbers of sad spectators leaving a stadium.

In modern football, the largest football crowd ever recorded was in the Michigan Stadium, USA, in 2014.

The super-sized American stadium filled up with about 109,000 spectators supporting Manchester United and Real Madrid, who were competing in the International Champions Cup. A big crowd for a friendly game.

The Most Amount of Goals Ever

Fans of other sports may knock football because of its lack of goals.

If you ever have to find yourself defending the excitement of our beautiful game, then perhaps point those other sports fans to this chapter.

The biggest winning margin in a game of football was 149-0. It happened in a match played between AS Adema and SO l'Emyrne of Madagascar in 2002. The Guinness Book of Records has it down as the world's biggest ever loss, but it never really was a 'competition'.

SO l'Emyrne threw the game by deliberately scoring own goals for 90 minutes. This was in protest against a disputed refereeing decision in the previous week's game. The poor referee at that game was powerless, and had to keep on blowing for the goal and re-starting play. For a whole hour and a half.

The game was meant to be a mouth-watering showdown between two ancient rivals, so the spectators demanded their money back after the game.

The local football association banned the coach and the captain of SO l'Emyrne for the rest of the season, and both teams (unfairly for one) got a severe reprimand.

The biggest scoreline, from a match where two professional* teams were actually competing, was delivered by Arbroath FC of Scotland.

They buried the hapless Bon Accord FC under 36 goals in the 1885 Scottish Cup. Bon Accord might have been outgunned, but at least they honourably tried to play.

In the modern era, though, the biggest drubbing on record happened in the South Pacific, when American Samoa lost their World Cup qualifier to Australia by 31-0 in 2002.

It was spectacular, but hardly a footballing spectacle. Australian Archie Thompson scored a world-record 13 goals in that match.

*paid footballers didn't come until much later, but they were compensated in other ways

Bury me in my Boots - I'll Never Hang Them Up!

Many footballers love the game too much to stop playing at a reasonable age.

It is very common to see fifty-year olds routinely lumber over marshy club fields on Sunday afternoons, occasionally embarrassing younger, less skilled players with defence splitting passes.

Still, nobody can hold a candle to Ezzeldin Bahader, the world's oldest professional football player who plays for Egyptian club October 6.

On March 7 2020, Bahader became the oldest active professional football player by coming onto the pitch at the grand old age 74 years and 125 days.

He missed a penalty in a 3-2 defeat to El Ayat Sports Club, but at least entered The Guinness Book of Records.

He also dislodged a disgruntled Isaak Hayik, who at 73, had been the previous record holder.

The following year, at 75, Bahader pushed new boundaries by scoring a professional goal for October 6 playing in the derby match against El Alyat.

Despite dizziness and a wonky knee, Bahader emerged from Covid-19 lockdown to play a full 90 minutes, and this time he managed to score from the spot.

Bahader might have retired from his job as a civil engineer, but his footballing career is still going strong at the time of writing.

With six grandchildren, he is never going to be short of supporters!

Football's Biggest Fraudster

Ali Dia could play football - just. He was much better at telling lies.

In 1996 he started ringing football clubs lying about who was. He claimed to be George Weah, who at the time was the world's best player. When he rang the clubs, he said that he had a cousin who played football really well and was looking for a club. He was essentially trying to sell himself.

Most football clubs rightfully dismissed the call as a hoax. But the phone then rang at Southampton FC and manager Graeme Souness picked up.

A few minutes later and we imagine the conversation went something like this:
Souness: "... Lastly George, you promise he's really good?"

"George Weah": "I promise. Why would I be saying this if he wasn't?"

What followed was one of the most bizarre tales in modern football.

Grame Souness, without seeing Ali Dia ever play, and simply going off a phone conversation with someone who claimed was the best football player on the planet, signed the midfielder on a one-month long contract.

In November 1996, and despite trepidations from the Southampton squad, Souness named Dia as a substitute for their game against Leeds.

After 32 minutes, Matt Le Tissier picked up an injury. Ali Dia was thrown on as a like-for-like substitute.

It was the worst appearance by a professional in the history of the sport. Dia was disastrous.

His teammates watched on, bemused and horrified as the obviously uncoordinated Dia stumbled and miskicked and, most disastrously, left the team severely handicapped.

Leeds scored. After 82 minutes Souness had had enough, and subbed him off for a real player. The damage had been done, and Leeds ended up winners at 2-0.

A Truly Golden Goal

Tahiti is a tiny country in the middle of the Pacific Ocean.

Its national team has very few full-time footballers. Most team members work in 9am-5pm professions, and go to football practice in the evenings.

In 2012, they had a golden season. They won the Oceania Football Confederation (a regional competition) and qualified for the 2013 Confederations Cup in Brazil!

They were going to be playing against the biggest teams in the world. And the question before all the encounters was simply about how little they could lose by.

In the end, Tahiti let in 24 goals in three matches, 6 against Nigeria, 10 against Spain, and 8 against Uruguay.

The most remarkable of their feats happened in the game against Nigeria: THEY SCORED A GOAL!

A towering header by one of the Tehau brothers sent everyone watching the tournament into delirium.

Every single neutral watched through teary eyes as the Tahitan players celebrated the moment of undiluted joy - despite being comprehensively beaten.

It clearly was a goal dedicated to everyone back in their home island. The Tahitans celebrated the goal by pretending to row in a canoe - in homage to their nation's fishing heritage.

A beautiful sight to behold and probably the most cheered on goal by fans everywhere across the globe (probably even Nigerians at that point - it was that emotional).

The team returned back home as heroes, having achieved an international competition goal.

Ice Cream, You Scream, We All Scream!

Football and ice cream are two of the BEST things in the world.

Sadly, they don't often combine.

Unless, of course, you were Stockport County in the 1920s!

Back then, football wasn't played professionally. Which means that no money was paid to players or for transfers of players between clubs.

In 1927, Manchester United liked the look of a certain player called Hugh McLenahan - he was playing for Stockport County.

United really wanted Stockport County to give them McLenahan. But as money wasn't allowed to be traded, they needed to come up with a different idea, an offer they couldn't refuse.

So United's assistant manager Luis Rocca, whose family business was in the ice cream industry, donated two freezers full of ice cream to Stockport County's fund-raising bazaar in exchange for McLenahan's services.

TWO FULL FREEZERS OF ICE CREAM!

No sane person in the world would refuse that offer! Stockport obviously accepted the offer, and off he went to play for United.

The Greatest Cup Run in The World

The story of Calais Racing Union FC is the Cinderella equivalent of amateur football fairy tales.

Some of the best feel-good stories in football are when part-time football players beat professional football players. But if there's one way to make a feel-good story feel even better, it's when the footballers who defeat the pros aren't part-timers, but complete amateurs.

That's exactly what happened in the 1999/2000 Coupe de France when Calais Racing Union had the best cup run any amateur side has ever seen. Their amazing run saw them beat Bordeaux in the semi-final and reach the final.

It was so exciting that even their manager had a minor heart attack and had to be briefly hospitalised! The president of France, Jacques Chirac, rang him up in hospital that evening to make sure he was OK.

The amateurs went onto the final at Stade De France, which had only recently been the venue for another final - the World Cup final!

Only Nantes stood between Calais and arguably the single greatest football story ever. Calais took the lead in the 34th minute of the game. We were about to see the unthinkable...

Unfortunately that's where the fairy tale stopped. Nantes went on to score two goals and win the game.

At the trophy presentation, the Nantes captain invited the Calais captain to accompany him. They lifted the trophy together in one of the most beautiful scenes competitive football had ever seen.

Calais had gained the hearts of the French nation - they were well and truly the people's champions.

THE MOST AMAZING SOCCER STORIES OF ALL TIME
BOOK 2 — FOR KIDS

Michael Langdon
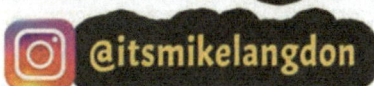
@itsmikelangdon

Illustrations by: Mihailo Tatic

Michael Langdon
© Copyright 2023 - All rights reserved.

The content contained within this book may not be reproduced, duplicated or transmitted without direct written permission from the author or the publisher.

Under no circumstances will any blame or legal responsibility be held against the publisher, or author, for any damages, reparation, or monetary loss due to the information contained within this book, either directly or indirectly.

Legal Notice:

This book is copyright protected. It is only for personal use. You cannot amend, distribute, sell, use, quote or paraphrase any part, or the content within this book, without the consent of the author or publisher.

Disclaimer Notice:

Please note the information contained within this document is for educational and entertainment purposes only. All effort has been executed to present accurate, up to date, reliable, complete information. No warranties of any kind are declared or implied. Readers acknowledge that the author is not engaged in the rendering of legal, financial, medical or professional advice. The content within this book has been derived from various sources. Please consult a licensed professional before attempting any techniques outlined in this book.

By reading this document, the reader agrees that under no circumstances is the author responsible for any losses, direct or indirect, that are incurred as a result of the use of the information contained within this document, including, but not limited to, errors, omissions, or inaccuracies.

Dedication

To Sarah:

A lifetime of gratitude and love
for supporting my maiden voyage into publishing.

Table of contents

The crowning of The GOAT	6
The Doe	8
More sendings off than players on the field!	10
The smell of disaster	12
Pain in the neck	14
The Kaiser	16
Sportsmanship gone too far	18
The wonderkid that never was	20
Brotherly love	22
A 5 month long game	24
The most confusing match ever!	26
Third bite of the cherry!	28
A fan's dream come true	30
The Bald Buddha	32

Shin pad superstitions	34
The most disastrous debut	36
The Hand of God	38
Winning a tournament they didn't qualify for!	40
Brazil's greatest humiliation	42
"Agüeroooooooooo...!!!"	44
The Invincibles	46
The Treble	48
The greatest comeback ever	50
Ghana take some time to recover from that!	52
Seeing red for seeing black	54
The Champions League that slipped away	56
Giants of the game	58
A Hat-trick of penalty misses!	60
Red card for the ref!	62
He misses more beautifully than others score	64

The crowning of The GOAT

Once upon a time, in the land of Qatar, the stage was set for the crowning of the soccer king - The Greatest Of All Time.

Lionel Messi was undoubtedly the best soccer player in the world, but to truly earn the title of The GOAT, he needed to win one specific trophy: The FIFA World Cup.

As his soccer superpowers were starting to wane, the 2022 World Cup was his final chance to win the prestigious event that only comes around once every four years. The weight of 45 million Argentineans rested squarely on his shoulders, and the pressure to perform well was immense.

Despite losing his first match, Messi's talent and perseverance shone through as he went on to score a goal at every stage of the World Cup. He single-handedly carried his team all the way to the final.

The final was the greatest the world had ever seen. The game ended in a 3-3 draw with France, and Messi scored two of the six goals. As the game ended in a draw, it had to be decided on penalties.

Lionel Messi's 20 years of tricks, goals, and mesmerizing dribbles were about to be recognized as the best ever, but only if the last penalty kick went in. His teammate Gonzalo Montiel stood on the penalty spot, and it all came down to that one kick of a soccer ball.

Montiel scored, and Messi, who was in the center circle, collapsed on his knees crying tears of joy. He had finally been crowned as the King of the Soccer World - the undoubted Greatest Of All Time.

The Doe

If we're going to talk about the male GOAT, we should also talk about the female GOAT.

(A doe is the name of a female goat in case you were wondering about the name of this chapter 😊)

In women's soccer we have someone who is so incredibly good, so outrageously talented, that she is the undisputed Greatest Of All Time.

Her name? Marta Vieira Da Silva of Brazil - simply known around the world as Marta.

She was the first soccer player of any gender to score at five World Cups, a feat which, in the men's game, has only recently been matched by Cristiano Ronaldo.

Marta is renowned for her grace on the ball, and the ease with which she can glide past any defender that tries to stop her. Watching her is the closest the world has come to actually witnessing poetry in motion.

The greatest accolade that can be given to Marta, on top of her being named Women's Player of the Year a record 6 times, is that she is the best to have ever played despite never winning the World Cup.

A very special mention must be given to the second greatest player of all time: Mia Hamm.

The American forward, who retired in 2004, remains in a class of her own. Most notably because of the decade she had in the 1990s, where she won two World Cups and two Olympic gold medals.

More sendings off than players on the field!

The scenes that followed Argentina's World Cup triumph after Lionel Messi's performance in 2022, showed us that the South American country is full of very passionate soccer people.

Sometimes this passion can be shown in moments of happiness or in moments of frustration.

Unfortunately for the teams of Claypole and Victoriano Arenas, their players were very passionately frustrated after a game in 2011.

After the game against Claypole, Victoriano Arenas players were not happy when the full time whistle was blown, and the mother of all fights broke out in the center circle. And it wasn't just the 22 players on the pitch getting involved.

Not wanting to be left out, along came the substitutes and the coaching staff of both teams to show their frustration.

Legend has it that even the bus drivers of the opposing teams got involved in the action!

In the aftermath of the storm, referee Damian Rubino walked into the dressing room of both teams to individually send off every single member of staff in each team.

That amounted to 36 red cards in total, and a Guinness Book of World Records award for the most sendings off in a single game of soccer!

The smell of disaster

The beautiful game has provided us with many funny tales. Whilst some of them are laugh-out-loud funny, others are peculiar.

Santiago Cañizares of Spain starred in one such tale in 2002. A story many found peculiar, but one that Cañizares himself certainly did NOT find funny.

The Spaniards were going through to the 2002 World Cup as one of the favorites.

Cañizares had just established himself as the Spanish number one goalkeeper, which at 32 years old, was somewhat late.

Whilst in his hotel room, days before flying to the World Cup, he headed into the bathroom to prepare himself for the night. That's when disaster struck!

His teammates heard a commotion from across the hall, and wanting to find out what had happened, they rushed to Cañizares' room only to be stopped by the doctors.

"Don't come in - there's glass everywhere" Doctors told his teammates.

Fearing the worst (like a break-in or an intruder) his teammates were somewhat relieved a few minutes later when they heard the news from the doctors.

It turned out that Cañizares accidentally knocked over a bottle of aftershave that was sitting on the bathroom sink.

The bottle smashed on the floor and broke into lots of tiny pieces and a couple of large shards.

Unfortunately for Spain's number one, one of those large shards flew into his foot and cut it really badly. He missed the World Cup and was out of action for a month.

How is that for the unluckiest injury in the history of the sport?

Pain in the neck

From an unlucky injury to probably the luckiest soccer player to survive an injury!

In the 1956 FA Cup final, Manchester City were playing Birmingham City at Wembley to decide the English Cup Champions.

With a quarter of an hour to play, a ball was played into City's box and a Birmingham striker nodded it down towards his oncoming teammate.

His teammate would have slotted it into the back of the net had it not been for the goalkeeper Bert Trautmann. Or to be more specific, Bert Trautmann's neck.

The running striker went, knee first, into Trautmann's neck, and whilst the keeper made the save, he lay motionless on the Wembley turf for a good few minutes.

He eventually got up whilst massaging his neck. A bit like when one sleeps at a funny angle and wakes up with a sore neck.

Trauttmann's neck wasn't sore. He had actually broken his neck in 5 places!

Luckily for Trautmann, English treatment for broken necks in the 1950s was world class. The coach rushed onto the pitch and fixed the injury by rubbing a wet sponge all over the keeper's face.

That allowed Trauttmann to keep playing in the game and become an FA Cup winner.

He would go on to collect his winners medal (still clutching his neck as if he'd had a bad sleep) from the Royal Box.

It was only a few days later, after the pain wouldn't go away that he went to the doctor and found out how bad his injury actually was!

The Kaiser

Another superhuman story of grit and resilience through injury (or just pure madness?!) goes to Trautmann's compatriot and one of history's very best players, Franz Beckenbauer. Also known as "The Kaiser".

In a World Cup semi-final game in 1970 he had one of his most incredible games. The game was dubbed "The Game of Century" - purely because it was a 4-3 thriller between two giants of the world game, Germany and Italy.

But on a personal level for Beckenbauer, what he did on the pitch that day defies belief.

After an early challenge by an Italian player, Beckenbauer landed awkwardly on his shoulder and broke his collarbone.

Any normal person would have gone straight to hospital, but not Der Kaiser.

Instead he ordered his medical team to bring a sling onto the pitch.

He placed his broken shoulder into the sling and continued to play for not only 90 minutes, but a whole 120 minutes, as the game went into extra time!

What makes Beckenbauer's performance so incredible is that he produced a masterclass of a display that day

In a world cup semi-final.

With a broken bone.

With his arm strapped to his chest.

In the center of the pitch!

The man, it would seem, was made from steel!

Sportsmanship gone too far

From a man made of steel to a man made of fluffy rainbows and unicorns.

Well, that's absolutely not the way anyone would describe Italian soccer player Paolo Di Canio, but there was one particular moment in his West Ham career that will go down in history.

West Ham were playing Everton and they were desperate for points.

There were 5 minutes left on the clock when an opportunity to clinch the 3 points - which they desperately needed - came West Ham's way.

A long ball was played into the Everton area and their goalkeeper, Paul Gerrard, was first to the ball to half clear it towards the corner flag. As he tried to run towards the ball to ensure it was fully cleared, he collapsed in agony clutching his leg. He had clearly injured himself.

With the keeper out of action 20 meters from his goal, the ball continued rolling towards the corner flag, where a West Ham player found it and fired a first time cross into the area.

The cross was remarkably accurate and heading towards one of the best strikers in the Premier League, Paolo Di Canio.

Di Canio was great at heading, volleying and scoring seemingly difficult goals, so whilst the ball was in the air and heading directly at him – and given that he was unmarked – everyone in that instant knew that it was going to end in the back of the net.

What happened next took everyone by surprise. Di Canio grabbed the ball with his hands and immediately told everyone to stop playing so that the Everton keeper could get some medical assistance.

His teammates were outraged, but the Everton players and fans applauded his selflessness.

To this day it remains one of the greatest fairplay gestures the world has ever seen!

The Wonderkid that never was

We've already spoken about Messi in Chapter One. The likes of him and Pelé come round once in a generation. Absolute beasts of the game who have no equals.

In between the eras of Pelé, Maradona and Messi/Ronaldo, there was one kid who was blessed with more natural ability than people had ever seen.

So much so, that he was given a $1 million sponsorship agreement by Nike at 14 years of age. That same year, he broke into the first team of DC United and scored his first professional goal.

All this a few months into becoming a teenager. He really was the real deal!

His name? Freddy Adu.

The American superstar was poised to become the greatest soccer player of all time. Just ask Pele who starred in a few television commercials with the 14 year old.

His progression continued, and at 16, he was training with Manchester United, under the watchful eye of the most successful British manager of all time, Sir Alex Ferguson.

Sadly, he didn't quite turn heads at Manchester United, and his career declined. In the end he never really played for a big club or won any major trophies.

He claims that his failure to reach the dizzying heights he was predicted was because clubs saw him as a marketing tool. It didn't allow him to nurture his talent and focus on his soccer career. However, the story does have a lovely ending.

Having had an unprivileged upbringing, all the money he made as a child went towards financially helping his mom, who had worked a few jobs after emigrating from Ghana to the USA to provide for her family.

Mother Adu never had to work again after Freddy turned 14.

Brotherly love

On June 23 2010 Ghana and Germany met in a World Cup match that made history for a very peculiar reason.

Brothers had often graced World Cup games and produced some real feel good family tales (from the Charlton Brothers winning the World Cup for England through to the De Boers for The Netherlands and the Laudrups for Denmark), but when Jerome and Kevin-Prince Boateng met in Johannesburg in 2010, they made headlines for very different reasons.

They were representing different countries!

Their father, Prince, moved to Germany from Ghana in 1981. A few years later he fathered Kevin-Prince with his first wife. After that marriage failed, he fathered Jerome with his second wife.

Both children would go on to represent Germany in soccer at youth level before Kevin-Prince switched allegiance and chose to represent Ghana. He had been unhappy about being left out of a U21 Germany squad and took the rash decision to change sides.

The two talented soccer players continued to rise through the ranks and play at the peak of the sport – and consequently they were selected by their nations to represent them.

When the draw for the World Cup in South Africa took place, all eyes turned to the Ghana VS Germany game as it would see brothers play against each other for the first time ever in a World Cup.

The game ended in a 1-0 victory to Germany courtesy of a Mesut Özil goal.

Curiously, the brothers would go on to line up against each other again at the following World Cup in Brazil.

Funnily enough, it is said by people close to the brothers, that George Boateng, the pair's older brother, was a much better soccer player than both Kevin-Prince and Jerome. Unfortunately for George, a troubled upbringing derailed his career..

A 5 month long game

On November 26 1898 referee Thomas Saywell accidentally blew for full time 10 minutes early in a match between Southampton FC and Millwall FC.

The mistake could not be immediately rectified by the referee as a pitch invasion occurred. So he proceeded to mark the game as over with the scoreline as it was. Millwall were losing so they were not happy about the decision.

So much so that they contested the referee's decision in a tribunal, and demanded that the remaining 10 minutes be played so that they had a fair chance of winning the game.

Nothing too unusual there apart from the fact that Millwall were losing 4-1 and had very little time to draw, let alone win, the match.

After 5 months of debate, the tribunal ruled in favor of Millwall. They decided that the last 10 minutes had to be played before the end of the season.

Southampton were forced to make the 160 mile return journey to London in April 1899 to play the last 10 minutes of a game that they surely had already won. A journey that (over 120 years ago!) must have been hard to make.

Begrudgingly they made their way to The Den to play those last 10 minutes. The result was one of the most incredible comebacks the world of soccer has ever seen....

...not really, those 10 minutes were the most boring 10 minutes of soccer ever seen, and the game still ended up being 4-1 to Southampton.

They went back to the south coast of England feeling like their time had been truly wasted, but at least the scoreline could be made official and Millwall could finally stop their whinging.

The most confusing match ever!

Winning a soccer game is simple: Put the ball in the opposing goal more times than your rival.

The sport becomes less simple when someone comes up with a rule that is so confusing, that it results in two competing teams trying their hardest to score own-goals!

This was the case in 1994, when Barbados and Grenada met in Concacaf's Shell Cup.

In an effort to increase the cup's popularity, the organizers imposed a rule which stated that a Golden Goal scored in extra time would not only win a match, but also count as two goals.

In the semi-final, Barbados needed to win by two clear goals to qualify for the final.

Barbados were leading 2-0 when, with 7 minutes of normal time remaining, Grenada scored to make it 2-1.

Barbados realized that they would be more likely to reach the final if they scored an own goal in the next 7 minutes, and then score a goal (worth two goals) in extra time.

What happened next was farcical: A Barbados defender shamelessly scored an obvious own goal.

The Grenadians realized that they needed one more goal at either end of the field to go through to the final (3-2 would see them win on points whilst 2-3 would see them win on goal difference).

The most unusual 3 minutes ever witnessed in international soccer followed.

Barbadians were defending their own goal as well as that of the opposition – the Grenadians were desperately trying to score at either but had no luck.

The game went into extra time, where Barbados scored the Golden Goal that counted for two. That took them through to the final of the 1994 Shell Cup final.

It's safe to say that that rule was never used again in a game of soccer.

Third bite of the cherry!

One of the least common offenses seen on a soccer pitch is players biting opponents. So when TV cameras capture three, and all of them are committed by the same player, you've got to question whether the player is simply just hungry!

Luis Suárez's first bite came in 2010 when he was playing for Ajax against PSV. There was a strong challenge in the middle of the pitch, and a small disagreement broke out.

It was during this disagreement that Suarez inexplicably bit Otman Bakkal in the shoulder. The referee missed it so Suarez went unpunished on the day.

However, the TV cameras did capture the incident, and after reviewing the footage, the Dutch Soccer Association suspended Suarez for 7 games.

Three years later, whilst playing for Liverpool FC, there was a coming together between Suárez and Chelsea's Branislav Ivanovic. The Chelsea defender was left rubbing his right arm in agony. Television replays showed that Suarez had taken a bite off of the defender's arm (again!).

Remarkably, this wasn't to be the last time he'd bite an opponent.

The next year he chomped on Giorgio Chiellini's shoulder during a World Cup game between Uruguay and Italy.

The referee again missed the action (he bites quickly!) but the cameras did pick it up.

Suárez claimed he was not responsible for the bite on Chiellini. Apparently he lost his balance and fell, teeth first, into Chiellini's shoulder.

A laughable excuse that makes you wonder whether he used the old " the dog ate my homework" excuse when he was at school.

After that third offense the Uruguayan was banned from all soccer-related activities for 4 months. That must have been hard to swallow.

A fan's dream come true

Steve Davies is an ardent fan of West Ham. And unfortunately for West Ham manager Harry Redknapp, Davies stood right behind his dugout on July 27 1994 when West Ham were playing a friendly game away to Oxford City.

Davies, an amateur soccer player, kept screaming his opinions to Harry Rednkapp on how he should be managing the team. As a matter of fact, he just wouldn't shut up about it, so Redknapp definitely noticed him on the day!

At the stroke of half time, Redknapp found himself a player down and with no available replacements on the bench. So he turned to the man that had been annoying him throughout the whole of the first half.

He strode over to the loud-mouthed fan behind the dugout and said "Oi, can you play as good as you talk?"

Next thing you know, Davies was being hustled down the tunnel to the changing rooms to be kitted out in the Claret & Blue. A few minutes later he came out and played for West Ham.

Davies was living the dream playing for the team he supported – and in the 71st minute it got even better: He scored a goal!

West Ham United went on to win 4-0 with Davies getting on the scoresheet for his boyhood club.

Unfortunately for the Hammers fan, West Ham didn't give Davies a contract.

They wouldn't even let him keep the shirt he played in, as the club needed it for their upcoming game against Newcastle!

The Bald Buddha

Some people avoid walking under ladders, others believe a smashed mirror signifies 7 years of bad luck.

Whatever crazy beliefs people may have, they probably don't measure up to the mad superstitions most soccer players have. And it seems to be everywhere in the game!

From wearing the same aftershave to games, the same socks, and rubbing certain players' bellies, we've seen it all on the soccer pitch.

One of the most iconic superstitions comes from the 1998 World Cup, and seemingly a very successful one as they ended up winning the whole tournament.

The superstition came from the French team and its main characters were Laurent Blanc and Fabien Barthez. On the way to World Cup victory, Blanc started a tradition of kissing the bald goalkeeper's head.

After the national anthems were sung, and before kick off, the defender would go over to his goalkeeper, firmly grab his face with two hands, pull the top of his head towards him, and give a kiss on his crown.

Quite the ridiculous theatrics. The only thing is, that the more they did it throughout the tournament, the more they won!

When they reached the final, which Blanc was suspended for, the whole of France was in a panic! How would they beat the Brazilians without that pre-match kiss?

Luckily for the whole nation, just before kick off and still in his tracksuit, Blanc came out of the dugout and kissed the goalkeeper on his head.

The whole of Brazil must have known it signified the impending doom.

Brazil did go on to have a shocker of a game — they lost 3-0 in the final.

The most superstitious of us still know it was all down to that lucky Blanc kiss.

Shin pad superstitions

Shin pads are an important part of the game. First and foremost, they keep players safe - having undoubtedly prevented many broken bones over the years.

Secondly, it would seem, many soccer players use them in superstitious rituals before a game.

England international soccer player Kyle Walker has worn the same shin pads every match day for the last 14 years. The defender, who earns over half a million dollars every month, has not once bought a new pair since he became a professional.

That's over 500 sweaty games that he's been wearing them for. "They will always be there. I will never change them" Walker has said. Apparently they still structurally resemble a shin pad – so they just about provide enough protection to his legs...

Another player who took superstitions to a new level was ex-England captain John Terry, who claimed to have had over 50 pre-match rituals. Much like Kyle Walker, he wore the same shin pads for over 10 years, and was devastated when he once lost them at Barcelona's Camp Nou.

So much so that he nearly had a panic attack thinking that the reason why they were 11 minutes from losing their following game (a cup final against Liverpool) was all down to the lost shin pads.

Terry's other superstitions included listening to the exact same songs every day before a match day and parking in exactly the same spot every time he drove to the stadium. He apparently went crazy for two hours before one particular game, when someone parked in his spot!

Another curious superstition came from Manchester United defender Phil Jones who would put his right sock on first if he was playing a home game and his left sock on first if the game was away.

The most disastrous debut

Ask any soccer fan about the worst debut in world history and they'll utter two words: Jonathan Woodgate.

The English defender was bought by Real Madrid from Newcastle in 2004. That's despite his previous season being riddled with injuries. So badly riddled with injuries that Real Madrid would not see him play for the club 13 months after they paid $13 million for him.

A million dollars for every month he laid in the physiotherapist's massage table!

By the time the 25-year-old's debut came, it had been 17 months since he had played soccer. Judging by his actions on the field that day, it looked more like it had been 17 years.

Woodgate must have been picturing a dream debut where he scored. And that's exactly what he did 25 minutes into the game. Unfortunately for Woodgate, it was an own goal!

Things couldn't get any worse for Woodgate... Or could they?

Within a minute of his teammates scoring two goals to counteract the one that Woodgate had scored against them, he got himself sent off!

You could be forgiven for thinking he was purposely trying to sabotage Real Madrid that day.

Madrid's "Galacticos" were made to sweat that day, and they once again saved Woodgate's bacon. They went on to score a third goal and Madrid won the game 3-1.

Woodgate's blushes will probably never be spared, as it's hard to imagine a worse debut for a club of that magnitude.

He never managed more than three appearances in a row for Real Madrid and went back to England, to the modest Middlesbrough FC, at the end of his maiden Spanish season.

The Hand of God

In 1986 England and Argentina met in the World Cup. Tensions were still running high from a war they had fought 4 years earlier.

The game was a knock-out quarter final game and two of the most remarkable things in World Cup history happened over the course of the following 90 minutes.

In the first half, a young Diego Maradona waltzed around the English back line before trying to play a one-two with his team mate. Maradona was so good that he got the English defender to play the one two for him - the defender accidentally looping the ball into the 6 yard box.

English goalkeeper Peter Shilton was just about to punch the ball away, when the little Argentinian magician jumped up and used his hand to nudge the ball into the back of the net.

An illegal move that was so audacious in nature that everyone in the ground was wondering why he was crazy enough to celebrate it like he was.

The problem was that the referee didn't spot the infringement and allowed the goal to stand.

Maradona didn't wait too long to admit his guilt. After the match he said it wasn't his hand that scored the goal, but rather "the hand of God".

To make matters worse for the English, four minutes later Maradona danced his way around half a dozen English players before slotting the ball past the English goalkeeper.

It was one of the most beautiful sights global soccer has ever seen. True poetry in motion. It became known as "The Goal of the Century".

It was something for the Argentineans to celebrate after a decade of disagreements with the English.

Winning a tournament they didn't qualify for!

At the end of June 1992 the Danish National side were flying back to Denmark with the Euro '92 trophy. But they had not even qualified to be there!

10 days before the tournament was due to start, Yugoslavia got disqualified because of international conflict. The Danes, who had come second in Yugoslavia's qualifying group, got catapulted into a group that contained Sweden, France and England.

Everyone (Danes included) thought they were there quite literally to fill an empty space left by the Yugoslavians. They drew against England in the first game.

Their second game saw them lose to Sweden, after which, the TV commentator famously said "Denmark are out of the European championship, how awful is that?".

The commentator was simply not expecting the Danes to beat the French team and the Swedes to beat World Cup semi-finalists England. And That's exactly what happened

Denmark were then up against The Netherlands, winners of the last European Championship. A side containing an almost incredible mix of legends of the game and upcoming talent.

The names of Rijkaard, De Boer, Koeman, Gullit, Bergkamp and Van Basten stood between Denmark and a place in the final. The game went to a penalty shootout after ending 2-2.

Danish goalkeeper Peter Schmeichel decided he was going to dive left for the first penalty in the shootout. Regardless of who was taking the first penalty.

Schemeichel became a world legend that day. He saved a penalty from Marco Van Basten and took his team to the final.

Denmark then beat giants Germany 2-0 in the final. The Danish minnows, who hadn't even qualified for the tournament, had just created history by winning Euro 1992.

Brazil's greatest humiliation

Brazilians, it seems, are born naturally being super talented at soccer.

Generation after generation they have thrived on the international stage, being the most successful team in the history of the sport with 5 World Cups.

So when they were playing at home in the semi-final of the 2014 World Cup - it was inevitable that they'd progress to the final. Then again, the Germans ain't bad at soccer either.

What Germany did to Brazil on the evening of July 8 2014 in Mineirão was torture.

They killed the joy of 200 million people. The collective happiness of a country sapped out of them in 90 fateful minutes.

Neither Germany nor Brazil had dropped a point on their way to the semi-finals. And the Brazilians were favorites to win the tournament given they were playing on home turf.

When the game kicked off, Brazil were quick off the traps and got a corner after 37 seconds. That would be as good as it got for them.

Before the half hour, Müller, Klose, Kroos (twice) and Khedira had put Germany 5-0 up. In scoring that goal, Klose overtook Ronaldo as the leading World Cup scorer in history.

Ronaldo himself was watching in the stands - talk about adding salt to the wound!

Schürrle scored another brace before full time to make it 7-0.

Poor old Oscar dos Santos Emboaba Júnior's goal in the 90th minute could not be considered a "consolation" goal.

Nothing could console the Brazilians after a 7-1 drubbing by Germany. No side had ever lost that badly in a World Cup semi-final.

Brazilians call it the Mineirazo, the Agony of Mineira. Funny that they named it because nobody in Brazil ever, ever speaks of it.

"Agüeroooooooooo...!!!"

There will never be a more dramatic final day of a Premier League season than the one witnessed in 2012.

Going into the beginning of the season, Manchester City had just won their first trophy in 35 years. It seemed the "noisy neighbors" of the most successful club in English history, Manchester United, were beginning to assert their dominance.

Both teams reached the final day of the season level on points.

City had a superior goal difference so it meant that going into the final day of the season they had to beat or match United's result to be crowned champions of England for the first time in 44 years.

Over in Sunderland, Manchester United beat the hosts - and as the game finished, United players were happy – they heard that City were losing 2-1 at The Etihad in the 90th minute.

There was plenty of injury time to be added on at the City game, and it was during this added time that 'The Miracle of Manchester' happened.

In the 92nd minute, Edin Dzeko headed in David Silva's corner!

At this point, The Red Devil's win over Sunderland still beat a Citizen's draw. The title was still United's.

But two minutes is a long time in soccer - and this is all it took for Aguero to take a shot at goal.
The shot rifled into the net and The Etihad went wild.

The commentator of the game howled an incredulous "Agüeroooooooooooooo...." that has now gone down in history as one of the most famous lines in British broadcasting history.

Manchester United were denied a 20th English crown in a cruel fashion, and Agüero forged his name into history books of Manchester City by almost single handedly earning City their first Top flight English crown in 44 years.

The Invincibles

In 2004 Arsenal achieved a feat that had only ever been achieved once before in English Top Flight soccer.

And it's a feat that has not been repeated since: Going a whole season without being defeated.

The only other team to have done it was Preston North End. But they did it in the 1888-1889 season, when it can be argued that it was an easier feat to achieve.

On the back of their unbeaten status, Arsene Wenger's boys won the Premier League in 2004 with 26 wins and a modest (although still impressive) 90 points.

As a result of that magic season, Gunners' fans often reminisce about The Invincibles.

That memorable season saw Thierry Henry lead the way in attack with 30 goals, which ended up being an impressive proportion of the Gunner's total of 73 goals.

Arsenal graced the league in the early noughties with the most exhilarating display of attackers which included Robert Pires, Freddy Ljunberg and Dennis Bergkamp.

Many note, though, that the defense played a huge role. Led by goalkeeper Jens Lehmann, the back line limited the opposition teams to a miserly 26 goals that season.

The truth is that The Invincibles were unbeatable simply because they had quality all over the pitch.

Arsenal went on to lift a special one-off golden edition of the Premier League trophy that season.

The Treble

Liverpool have been there or thereabouts. Manchester City have missed it by a whisker. The Invincibles of 2004 didn't even get near it. It's an almost impossible feat to achieve.

Only one English team has ever won what most consider the most elusive of soccer records: Winning The Premier League, The UEFA Champions League and the Football (soccer) Association Cup in one season.

In 1999, Manchester United did just that. And they did it in one of the most dramatic fashions The Champions League has ever seen.

Having been crowned domestic League and Cup Champions earlier in the month, Manchester United went into the Camp Nou in Barcelona, on the 26th May 1999, knowing that a victory against Bayern Munich would seal their fate as immortals of the game.

They were up against it in Barcelona. And it showed.

For 89 minutes in the final, United players were very average. They were lucky to only be losing 1-0.

But in the 90th minute, David Beckham took a corner. Sheringham scored from it.

In the 92nd minute, Beckham did his thing again and, with literally only a dozen or so seconds left on the clock, Solskjaer scored from Beckham's corner. The most incredible scenes followed.

United had won the Treble in the most dramatic of ways!

Solskjaer ran to the corner and slid on his knees in jubilation. He had just made history.

The world would never see such drama in a final again, until 6 years later in Istanbul when AC Milan and Liverpool met...

The greatest comeback ever

AC Milan were cruising to victory in the UEFA Champions League Final of 2005. They were 3-0 up at half time, and their opponents, Liverpool, were simply outgunned.

As the players trudged back to their dressing rooms, neutral fans couldn't help but feel a sense of embarrassment for the Liverpool players.

What AC Milan had done in the initial 45 minutes was undone in 7 second half minutes by Liverpool.

Captain Steven Gerrard, scored his first headed goal for the club in four years. What a time to break that run. He inspired Vladimir Smicer to score a second two minutes later, before being brought down in the box by Gennaro Gattuso and earning Liverpool a penalty kick. Xabi Alonso tucked it away.

AC Milan capitulated and Liverpool found themselves back in the game.

After a few near misses by AC Milan, the teams found themselves going into a penalty shootout after 120 minutes of soccer played. All was set for the goalkeepers to shine. The Dudek-Dida show.

Dudek most certainly stole the show. Not just because of his dancing antics on the goalline as the opposition lined up to take penalties, but because he saved a penalty from dead ball specialist Andrea Pirlo.

At 3-2 a piece in the penalty shootout, the European Soccer Player Of The Year, Andriy Shevchenko, stepped up. His meek penalty was saved by Dudek and mayhem ensued in Istanbul. Liverpool had just won the trophy after being 3-0 down at half time.

The unlikeliest of comebacks had just taken place. Liverpool gave the world a lesson in grit, determination and perseverance that evening, and sealed a much deserved victory in the Champions League.

Ghana take some time to recover from that!

The first ever World Cup to be hosted in Africa took place in the summer of 2010.

The Ghanaians had a golden generation of a team and they were the undoubted people's favorite as the tournament progressed.

They were seconds away from making it to the semi-final, had it not been for the most dramatic act of dishonesty a World Cup has ever seen.

Ghana and Uruguay were tied at 1-1 and the game went into extra time. In the last minute of extra time, there was a mad scramble in the Uruguayan's box.

In an act of defending desperation, Luis Suarez stopped the Ghanaians from scoring by punching the ball away from his goal line.

For those unfamiliar with the name, Luis Suarez was NOT the Uruguayan goalkeeper. He was Uruguay's striker, and he had just committed the most fragrant and obvious act of cheating the world had ever seen. (What would Paolo Di Canio think?!)

Ghana would have won the game had Suarez not cheated. Instead, they got compensation in the form of a penalty kick.

It was the last kick of the game and they were given the chance to win the game if they scored that penalty kick.

Up stepped Asamoah Gyan who rocketed his shot against the crossbar. Suarez, who was watching from the tunnel (he had been sent off for cheating) celebrated as if he'd just won the World Cup.

It was the most unjust and dramatic quarter final the world had ever seen. The people's champions had been swindled out of a semi-final spot in the first world cup held in their continent.

Ghana went on to lose the game on penalties. Gyan, understandably, was inconsolable after the game. The Uruguayans celebrated wildly into the night.

Seeing red for seeing black

There is a player in Argentina who could well be right in thinking that he's the unluckiest recipient of a red card in the history of the game.

Juan Pablo Krilanovich was playing a game for Lanus Reserves as a midfielder. The tactics were simple from the coach: Apply pressure everywhere on the pitch. Something straight out of the Jurgen Klopp book of coaching.

So when the midfielder was high up the field, applying pressure on the back line of Banfield Reserves, Banfield central defender Lautaro Cardozo panicked.

The age old saying of "when in doubt, kick it out!", came straight to him, and that's exactly what he did. He booted the ball as hard as he could.

Unfortunately for Kirlanovich, he was doing his job of pressing so well (and so quickly!), that his face was right in the way of the defender's clearance.

The ball hit Kirlanovich's face, making him lose consciousness. As a result, his legs stopped functioning properly, and with momentum still in full force, he stumbled towards his opponent.

The midfielder landed awkwardly on the opposition's leg and twisted the defender's knee. Two players out for the count.

One with a suspected twisted knee, and the other with a concussion.

Kirlanovich's concussion didn't last long - he woke up a couple of minutes later and was given a red card by the referee for his clumsy challenge on Cardozo, which unfortunately, did break the defender's leg.

To the best of our knowledge, it's the first red card for an unconscious incident on a soccer pitch.

You can just about hear Kirlanovich's pleading: "But Ref, I was UNCONSCIOUS!"

The Champions League that slipped away

One of the unluckiest moments on a soccer pitch happened on a wet Moscow evening in 2008.

Manchester United and Chelsea had gone head-to-head in the Premier League that season, with United just coming out on top after the last game of the season.

So when the teams met in the final of the Champions League, it couldn't have been a closer affair. The game ended 1-1 and went to penalties. Didier Drogba, one of their main penalty takers, had been sent off in extra time, so he wouldn't have the opportunity to take a penalty.

A very unusual occurrence happened during the shootout: Cristiano Ronaldo missed his penalty. And he missed that penalty in the last game of a season where he had scored 42 goals (including one in that very final!).

It was extremely surprising and unusual. But such is life. The world's best player had, somewhat ironically, cost Manchester United the chance to win the world's biggest club trophy. Or so it seemed…

John Terry stood 12 yards from goal ready to kick into a net only guarded by Edwin Van Der Sar.

Score the penalty and Chelsea win the Champions League. Easy as that.

As John Terry took his kick (Van Der Sar diving the opposite way to the ball), he slipped on the wet Moscow grass and his shot hit the post.

Manchester United not only got back into the shootout but ended up winning the game, lifting the Champions League trophy.

John Terry cut a desolate figure as he left the pitch in tears.

Had Dider Drogba been on the pitch, he probably would have taken the deciding penalty (like he did in Munich 4 years later) and won the game for Chelsea. Without doubt the unluckiest slip of all time.

Giants of the game

Soccer tends to be a sport for the quick and flexible, with height being a particular advantage for defenders and strikers.

The game, nonetheless, has had some behemoths on the pitch, men who in other circumstances would have been snapped up as offensive linemen for their local American Football team.

Micky Quinn, born in 1962, was one of those players whose muscular frame eventually ran him into weight issues.

He was, however, a force to be reckoned with, scoring 227 goals in his 535-game professional career.

In his prime, at 88 kg in weight, he was still doing the job. Fans would cheer him on by singing — "He's fat, he's round, he scores at every ground, Micky Quinn, Micky Quinn!"

Opposing fans were less kind, but that did not stop him scoring goals.

However, The King of Timber award in our list of soccer heavies goes to William Foulke.

Foulke, a goalkeeper, filled the goalmouth at 1.9m and 150kg by the end of his professional career.

Foulke won a cap for England in 1897 and played most of his long career for Sheffield United.

He truly was the monster of all monsters, yet surprisingly limber, despite his tonnage.

In fact, he was so limber, that he also played professional cricket during his career!

A Hat-trick of penalty misses!

In 1999 Martin Palermo delivered a performance that defied all odds. It was the group stages of the Copa America, and Argentina were favorites to beat Colombia and top their group.

Five minutes had passed in the game, when a Colombian defender handled the ball in the box. Penalty to Argentina.

Palermo confidently stepped up to the spot and slammed an unstoppable missile into the crossbar — making the ball bounce away into the stands.

It was early. There was plenty of time for it to get worse for Palermo.

Colombia took the lead and shortly after that Argentina got awarded yet another penalty kick.

Funnily enough the same defender handled the ball in the area again. Redemption time for Palermo!

He stepped up and spun the ball into place on the spot. He walked back about half a kilometer, sprinted in and...fired the ball over the crossbar!

With 90 minutes on the clock, Colombia were leading 3-0. The game was well and truly finished, so when Palermo got fouled in the Colombian penalty area and won a penalty kick. He quickly dusted himself off, grabbed the soccer ball and placed it on the spot.

Surely that was the only thing the Argentinians would rescue from the match. Palermo had the chance to atone his two previous penalty misses.

So with arguably the most important thing to play for in his career, his dignity, he took a couple of steps back and took the penalty.

Colombian goalkeeper, Miguel Calero, guessed the direction of the kick and the ball went straight into his midriff. The full time whistle was blown seconds later and Calero joined in the Colombian celebrations!

Palermo is the only holder of this "anti-hat-trick" in soccer, a record three penalties fluffed in an international encounter.

Red card for the ref!

Referee Graham Poll delivered a shocker of a performance in 2006. So much so, that it ended his international whistle-blowing career.

The game was Australia vs Croatia, and in fairness to Poll, he blew an impeccable first half. It was Poll's second half that left a lot to be desired...

In the 61st minute of the game, Croatian defender, Josip Šimunić, was yellow carded for bringing Harry Kewell down in the edge of the box.

The game was tied at 2-2 with a few minutes to go, and things were getting breathless.

Just before stoppage time, Šimunić knocked down an Australian attacker in the area. Poll blew for the penalty and awarded Šimunić another yellow card.

The world stood still, waiting for Poll to show Šimunić the mandatory red that follows two yellow cards... only that never happened!

Poll forgot that Šimunić had been previously booked and failed to send him off. Play continued.

After the game, the referee admitted that he had written the previous yellow card under another player's number in his book, and that's why the second yellow never turned into a red.

As soon as Šimunić realized his luck, you would have thought that he would hide himself away on the field somewhere.

Quite the opposite happened. Šimunić wasn't very good at hiding himself away on the field, and in the 93rd minute, with justice prevailing (or silliness prevailing, it depends on who you ask), Šimunić started arguing with the referee and got booked (for the third time!) for dissent.

Imagine riding your luck that badly that you show dissent after having already been booked twice!

Third time was the charm for Poll, and on that occasion, he rightfully did remember to send the player off!

He misses more beautifully than others score

When a nice move on the pitch doesn't result in a goal, it is often quickly forgotten. But not in the case of The King, Pelé, who 'scored' the greatest goal that never was.

When he missed the goal, the world took notice. The things he did with his body in the lead up to that miss had never been seen before in the world of soccer.

So how exactly did the most beautiful miss *ever* unfold? It happened in the 1970 World Cup when Brazil were playing Uruguay.

Tostao stole the ball from a Uruguayan player and played a delightful, perfectly weighted through ball to Pelé.

Pelé accelerated towards the ball at the same time as the Uruguayan keeper was. It seemed as if they were both going to get to the ball at exactly the same time.

It seemed inevitable that they were both going to collide on the edge of the box. But in a second that seemed a lifetime, Pelé did nothing but let the ball run past him.

No one does 'nothing' more elegantly than The King. For that split second he danced, played and mesmerized. Danced with the ball, toyed with the keeper, and mesmerized millions.

Pelé's clever maneuver led to the keeper finding himself 25 yards out of his goal, with ZERO clue as to where the ball was. Talk about looking silly!

Pelé knew exactly what he was doing, and without even touching the ball, found himself with an open goal from a tight angle.

He took his shot, and incredibly, the ball trickled a few yards wide from the post.

The game changed that day, however. The greatest miss of all time showed us all that soccer was not a game of brute force, but indeed was The Beautiful Game.

A quick favor

Reviews are the bedrock of my success. Taking 5 minutes of your time to review this book will benefit me in one of two ways.

If the book wasn't to your satisfaction, please leave constructive criticism to make me a better author.

If you enjoyed the book, a good review will give my book more clout in the Amazon algorithms and generate more exposure for my books. I'd be extremely grateful if you could rate my book now.

Thank you.

Instagram: @itsmikelangdon

By The Same Author

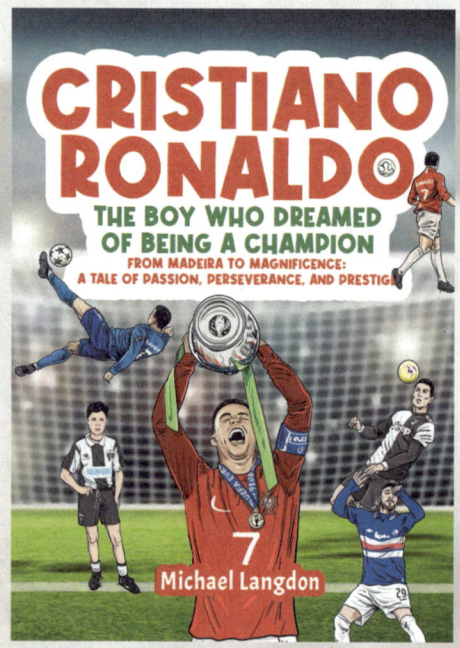
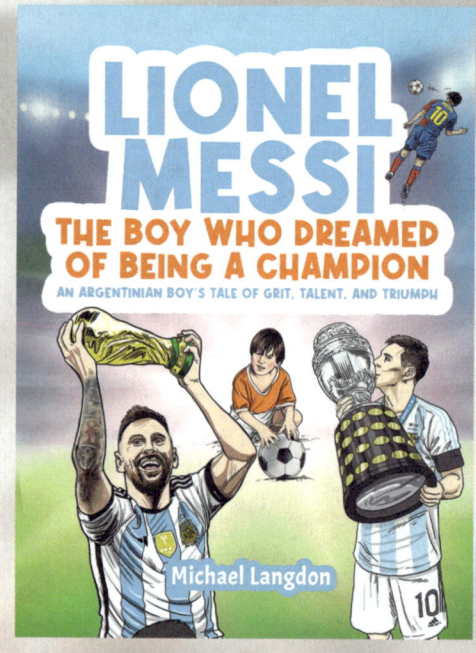
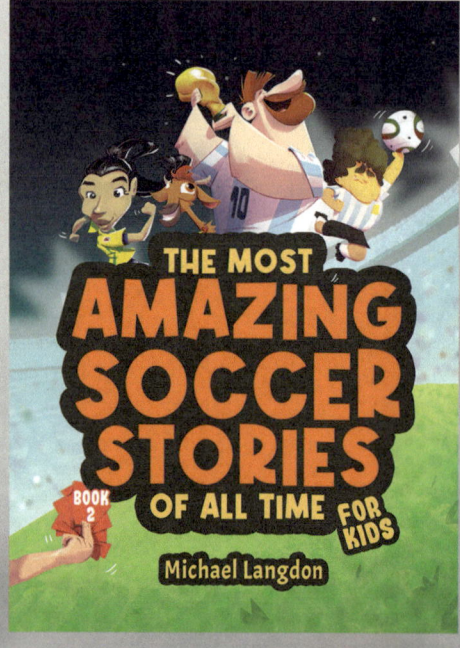
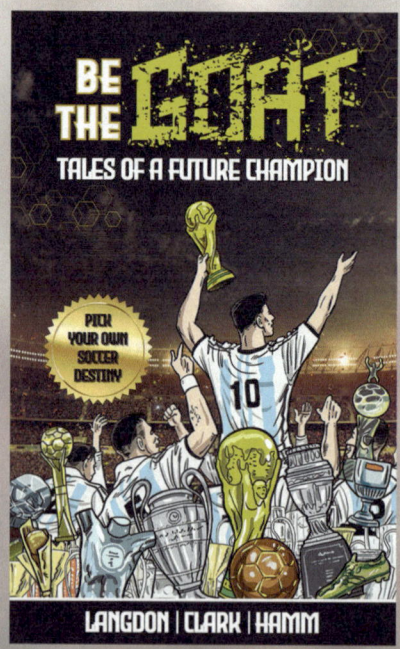

Made in United States
Troutdale, OR
11/07/2024